THE BIGGEST EVER BOOK OF ORIGAMI

THE
BIGGEST
EVER
BOOK OF
ORIGAMI

with 12 giant templates

Nick Robinson

Ivy Press

First published in the UK in 2009 by

Ivy Press

210 High Street, Lewes
East Sussex BN7 2NS
United Kingdom
www.ivy-group.co.uk

British Library Cataloguing-in-Publication Data
A catalogue record for this book is available from the British Library

ISBN: 978-1-905695-85-0

Ivy Press

This book was conceived, designed and produced by Ivy Press
Creative Director Peter Bridgewater
Publisher Jason Hook
Editorial Director Tom Kitch
Art Director Wayne Blades
Designers Kate Haynes and Andrew Milne
Photographer Neal Grundy

The designs were created by Wayne Brown (yacht), Sy Chen (pencil
holder), Edwin Corrie (duck), Rudolf Deeg (mirror fish), Francesco
Guatnieri (rosetta), Stephen O'Hanlon (rabbit), Tony O'Hare (frog),
Mark Leonard (pteranodon), Robert Neale (raven mask), Nick Robinson
(box and elephant) and Leyla Torres (inflatable chicken).

The author would like to thank his wife Alison, David Petty for
proofing the diagrams, the British Origami Society for encouragement,
and all at Ivy Press for making this book happen. The author's website
is www.origami.me.uk - please get in touch if you enjoy this book or
have any origami questions.

Picture Acknowledgements
The prints featured on pages 6, 9, 13, 17, 19 and 23 are reproductions
of woodblocks by Katsushika Hokusai, first published as a collection
in *Thirty-Six Views of Mount Fuji* (1831). Digital reproductions are courtesy
of the Library of Congress, Washington, DC.

Printed and bound in China

10 9 8 7 6 5 4 3 2 1

contents

*O*rigami is the Japanese word for 'folding paper'. The art has been around for over 2,000 years, starting in the East and spreading around the world during the last few hundred years. Nowadays, the Internet has led to a huge interest in paper folding and people regularly put up photos of new models and diagrams showing how to fold them. It's a hobby that requires very little money - all you need is a sheet of paper. People will be so impressed when you make a model for them; it's always nice to receive a homemade gift.

using this book

We suggest that you learn the basic designs using squares made from ordinary paper. Once you can fold them well, use the giant templates in the book. The designs are presented in order of difficulty, so it is wise to fold them in order and not be tempted to start with the last one, however exciting it looks.

Always fold slowly and don't flatten the folds until the paper is perfectly in position. Fold on a large, clear table, with plenty of light to see what you are doing. It's double the fun to fold with a friend and you will be able to help each other through the slightly trickier steps. Please read the section on folding symbols before you start - it will help. Also, don't forget to read both the diagrams and the words for each project.

biggest origami

There are many ways in which you can continue to have fun with origami after you've folded the models in this book. The projects include creative tips which suggest new ideas for experimenting with the folding instructions to modify the final models. Another fun idea is to buy even bigger sheets of patterned or coloured paper to see how large you can make the projects in the book.

If you really enjoy folding, why not join an origami society? Two really great ones are Origami USA (www. origami-usa.org) and the British Origami Society (www.britishorigami.info). If you go to school, they are sure to be delighted to help you form an origami club so you can fold during your lunch break.

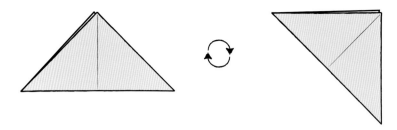

rotate

Turn the paper 90 degrees in the direction of the arrows.

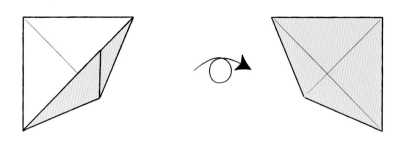

turn over

Turn the paper upside down, like flipping a pancake.

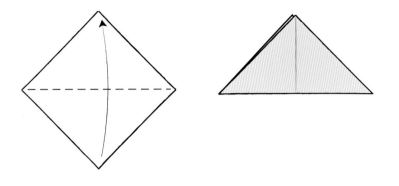

valley fold

Fold the paper in the direction of the arrow. Take your time to line the edges up neatly. Hold the paper in place with one hand and put in the crease with the other.

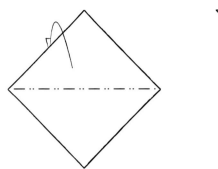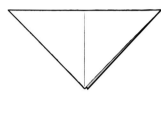

mountain fold

The paper is folding underneath. It's actually easiest to turn the paper over and make a valley fold, but remember to turn it back over so the diagrams match the paper.

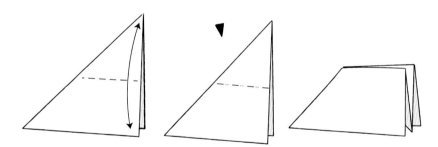

inside reverse (push in)

A folded corner is pressed inside the paper. Make the initial crease as a valley, then change the creases as shown, opening the body slightly and gently pushing the corner inside.

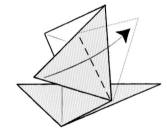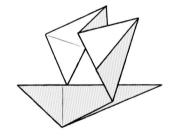

fold to the dotted line

Use the dotted line as a guide to where to fold.

folding symbols

If you learn these few simple symbols, you will be able to make the models without even needing the words. They will also allow you to understand 'normal' origami diagrams.

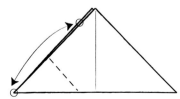

fold between circled points

The circles show exactly where the points should meet.

 15–18

repeat indicated steps on the other side

Follow the same sequence as before on the other side.

7

yacht

design by Wayne Brown

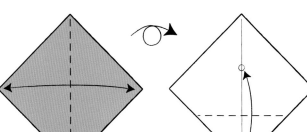 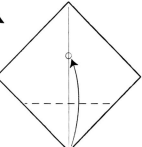 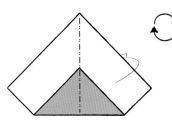 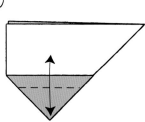 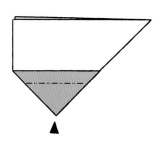

1 Start with a square, patterned side upward. Fold side to side, crease and unfold.

2 Turn the paper over. Fold the lower corner to a point about two-thirds along the diagonal.

3 Mountain-fold in half behind.

4 Rotate the paper to this position. Fold over three-quarters of the patterned triangular flap, crease and unfold.

5 Inside-reverse the lower corner.

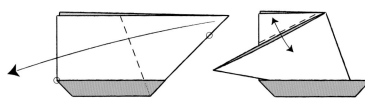 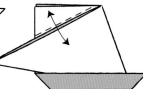 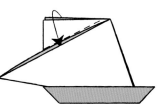 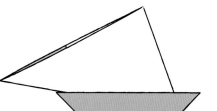

6 Fold the plain corner to the left so that the circled points meet.

7 Fold the small plain section over the edges, crease and unfold.

8 Refold the flaps, tucking them between the layers of the sail.

9 The yacht is finished.

*t*his design has a sail that extends beyond the stern of the boat, which is quite unusual in origami. At step 5, you will make an inside reverse fold (see page 7). This is a common move in origami, but it can sometimes confuse beginners. Essentially, the lower corner is being pressed upwards so it folds symmetrically inside the paper. When you have managed the step, open the paper out slightly and flex the model until you see exactly what has happened. After this, you should have no trouble with this technique.

creative tip

The 'pre-crease' for the reverse fold is made in step 4. It's not vital where you make the crease - what happens if you make it higher or lower than shown?

pencil holder

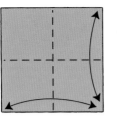 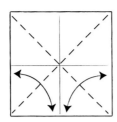 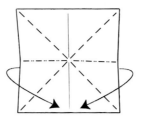 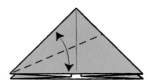 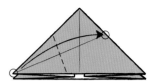

1 Start with a square, patterned side upward. Fold side to opposite side, crease and unfold. Repeat with the other sides.

2 Turn the paper over. Crease and unfold both diagonals.

3 Using only the existing creases, collapse the paper towards you.

4 Fold the upper left edge to the bottom edge, crease and unfold.

5 Fold the first corner on the left to the end of the crease you've just made.

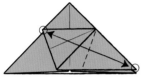  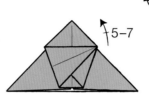 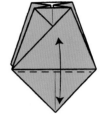 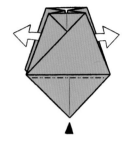

6 Fold the first right corner to the circled point, crease and unfold.

7 Refold the flap, tucking it into the pocket.

8 Repeat steps 5 to 7 on the opposite side.

9 Rotate the paper 180 degrees. Fold the lower triangular flap over, crease and unfold.

10 Open the model by putting your fingers inside and gently pressing it out. Flatten the lower corner to form the base.

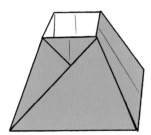

11 The pencil holder is finished.

Origami designs can be practical as well as decorative – here's a useful container for pencils, incense or anything else that will fit. The first three steps produce a well-known origami base known as the 'waterbomb' base. You'll often meet it in other designs, so try to memorize the sequence.

creative tip

In step 5, try folding the corner not quite to the end of the crease. At what point does step 7 stop working?

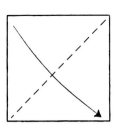

1 Start with a square, plain side upward. Fold the top left corner to the bottom right corner.

2 Fold the lower left corner to the right.

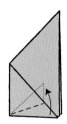

3 Fold the corner upwards to match the dotted line.

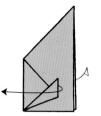

4 Open the paper out to match the next drawing.

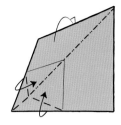

5 Form an outside reverse fold using the creases shown. The tail wraps around the outside as the paper closes.

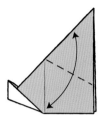

6 Take the folded edge to lie on the vertical crease. Crease firmly and unfold.

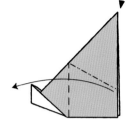

7 Fold the upper layer to the left, flattening the top flap downwards as you go.

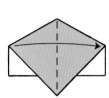

8 This is the result. Fold in half from left to right.

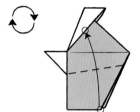

9 Rotate the paper to this position. Fold the lower corner of the wing to meet the circled point.

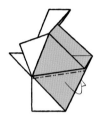

10 This is the result. Repeat the move on the underside.

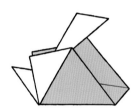

11 The duck is finished.

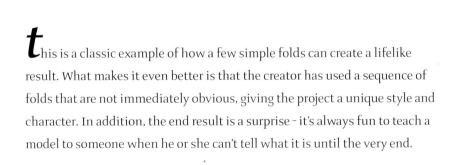

this is a classic example of how a few simple folds can create a lifelike result. What makes it even better is that the creator has used a sequence of folds that are not immediately obvious, giving the project a unique style and character. In addition, the end result is a surprise - it's always fun to teach a model to someone when he or she can't tell what it is until the very end.

creative tip

Vary the angle used to create the wings in step 9 - does it make it look more like a duck, or less?

mirror fish

design by Rudolf Deeg

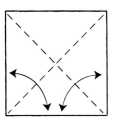 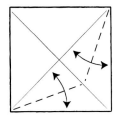 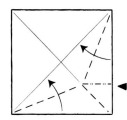 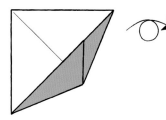 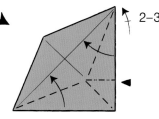

1 Start with a square, plain side upward. Fold corner to opposite corner, crease firmly and unfold. Repeat with the other corners.

2 Fold the lower and right edges to the diagonal crease, but only make the crease up to the other diagonal. Crease and unfold.

3 Fold the two sides in at the same time, forming a small triangular flap in the centre which you flatten to the right.

4 This is the result.

5 Turn the paper over and rotate it to the position shown. Repeat steps 2 and 3 on this side.

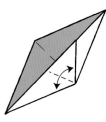 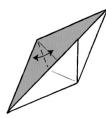 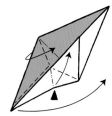 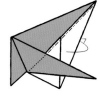 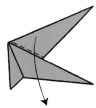

6 Fold the lower edge to meet the inside folded edge. Crease and unfold.

7 Make a matching fold on the other side.

8 Make three valley creases to form a three-dimensional point. Swing this to the right and flatten to form a mountain crease.

9 Mountain-fold the plain section underneath.

10 Fold the narrow flap downwards.

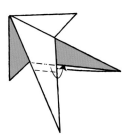 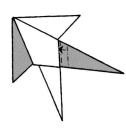 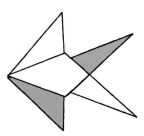

11 Make a small pleat and tuck it in between two layers.

12 Repeat on the other tail fin. This is slightly harder than the earlier move, but fold carefully and you'll get there.

13 The mirror fish is finished.

*t*his model exploits the different colours and patterns on a typical sheet of origami paper to make an eye-catching design. The model itself uses a variation of the 'fish base' in which, unusually, each half of the model folds to opposite sides. You'll need to be careful with step 12, easing the paper apart to slide in the flap.

creative tip

Can you apply this idea to any other models in the book? Both the raven mask and the pteranodon use the fish base.

elephant

design by Nick Robinson

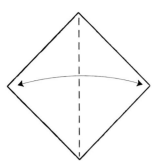

1 Start with a square, plain side upward. Crease from corner to corner and unfold.

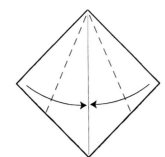

2 Fold the two upper edges to the vertical centre crease.

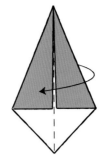

3 Fold in half from right to left.

4 Fold the lower corner over (see step 5).

5 Fold the inner point back out (see step 6).

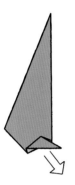

6 Unfold the point.

7 Make two reverse folds, pushing the corner in and back out again.

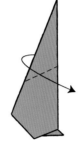

8 Fold the upper flap over (see step 9).

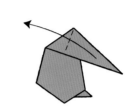

9 Fold the flap back over - the angle isn't critical.

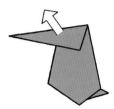

10 Unfold the point.

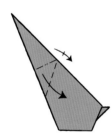

11 Make the creases shown on both sides at the same time, spreading the flap outwards.

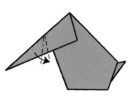

12 Make a pleat in the paper to form the trunk.

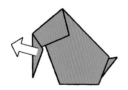

13 Unfold the last step.

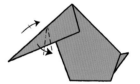

14 Form the trunk in the same way as in step 11.

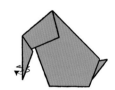

15 Wrap the end of the trunk around. The elephant is finished.

*t*hese animals are an ideal challenge for origami creators; all you need to make is a trunk, ears and a large body. Very few of these models actually look like a real elephant, but they have a recognizable form. The move at steps 11 and 14 is known as a 'crimp' and takes a little practice, but it is a technique that you will find used in many origami designs.

creative tips

By altering the angles and proportions of both the head and the tail, you can create many different variations - find the one that says 'elephant' most strongly to you. You could try 'blunting' the tip of the trunk by folding the tip back inside.

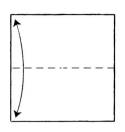

1 Start with a square, plain side upward. Fold in half from bottom to top, crease and unfold.

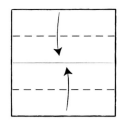

2 Fold the upper and lower edges to the centre.

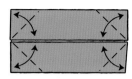

3 Fold each corner to the centre, crease and unfold.

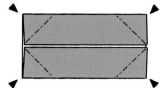

4 Inside-reverse each of the corners.

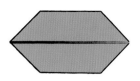

5 This is the result.

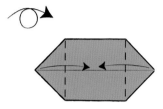

6 Turn the paper over. Fold the upper corner on either side to the centre.

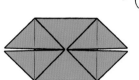

7 This is the result.

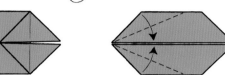

8 Turn the paper over. Fold the edges on the left to meet the horizontal centre.

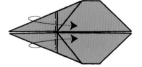

9 Fold the narrow flaps on the left over to the right, allowing a flap to flip round to the left.

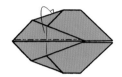

10 Fold the upper half behind.

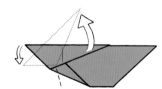

11 Hold the 'ear flaps' and ease them upwards. At the same time, ease the nose downwards to match the dotted line. The valley crease shown extends inside the model to the top. When the paper is in position, flatten it so that it stays there.

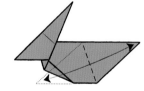

12 Fold the right corner across so it lines up with the lower horizontal edge. Crease and unfold.

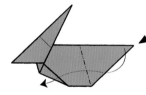

13 Inside-reverse the same flap.

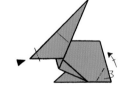

14 Fold the two lower right corners inside to shape the body. Inside-reverse a small section on the left to shape the nose.

15 The rabbit is finished.

*a*s in nature, there are plenty of origami rabbits - and in origami terms, some of them share 'genes'. This design was created independently yet has techniques in common with other rabbit designs. Origami is a huge melting pot of techniques and almost every new design that arises is in some way built upon creative work from the past.

creative tip

The model in step 5 is a variation of the 'multiform base'. Try experimenting to find other ways of making and using this base.

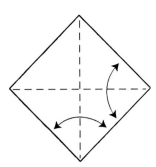

1 Start with a square, plain side upward. Fold in half from corner to opposite corner, crease and unfold. Repeat the opposite way.

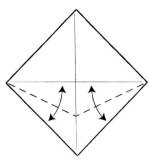

2 Fold each lower edge to the horizontal crease. Crease only as far as the vertical crease. Unfold again.

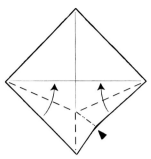

3 Fold in using the three valley folds to form a small triangular flap. Flatten this flap to the right - this forms the mountain crease automatically.

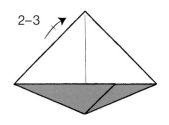

4 Repeat the last two steps on the opposite corner.

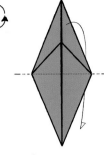

5 Rotate the paper counter-clockwise to this position. Fold the top corner in half behind.

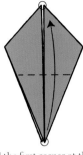

6 Fold the first corner at the bottom in half to the top corner.

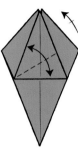

7 On the upper triangular flap, fold the left edge to the bottom edge, bisecting the corner angle. Crease and unfold. Repeat from the opposite side.

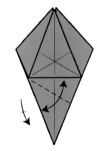

8 Make the same two creases on the lower section.

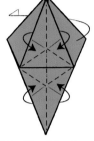

9 Fold the sides of the triangular flaps forward using a slight variation of the technique used in step 3. As you do so, mountain-fold the upper section behind to the left (see step 10).

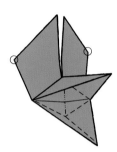

10 Here's the move in progress. The circled corners meet behind.

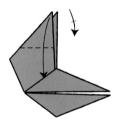

11 Fold the flap down on the valley crease, then tuck the lower corner behind a layer. Repeat underneath.

12 The raven mask is finished.

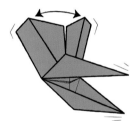

13 Open and close the two rear corners to open and close the mouth.

*t*his origami design falls into the category of 'action model' - in other words, it 'does' something. In this case, the beak opens and closes as you hold the sides of the head and move your hands. Like many origami animals, the folding method is neat and symmetrical - every fold you make on one side of the diagonal, you must also make on the other side.

creative tip

Step 6 determines the size of the beak. Fold the flap past the corner or so that it doesn't quite meet it and see how it affects the finished result.

pteranodon

design by Mark Leonard

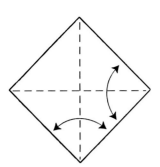

1 Start with a square, plain side upward. Crease and unfold both diagonals.

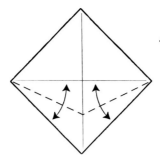

2 Fold each lower edge to the horizontal diagonal. Crease only as far as the vertical diagonal and unfold.

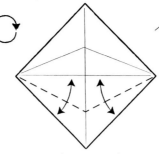

3 Rotate the paper 180 degrees and repeat step 2.

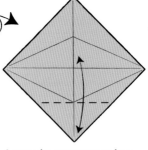

4 Turn the paper over. Make a horizontal valley crease through the intersection of the most recent creases.

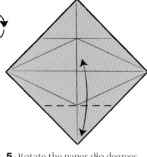

5 Rotate the paper 180 degrees and repeat step 4.

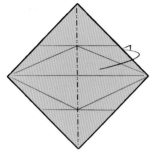

6 Mountain-fold the right-hand half behind.

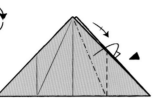

7 Rotate to this position and make the folds shown on both sides of the paper at the same time.

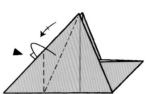

8 This is the result. Repeat on the left-hand side.

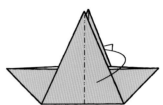

9 Fold the right-hand half behind.

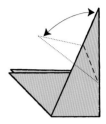

10 Fold the narrow point over to match the dotted line. Crease and unfold.

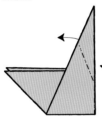

11 Make an inside reverse fold using the crease made in the step 10.

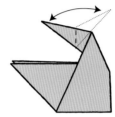

12 Fold the point over again so that the lower edge touches the corner. Crease and unfold.

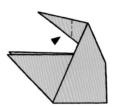

13 Make an inside reverse fold using the crease made in step 12.

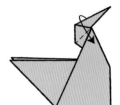

14 Fold down half of the head flap.

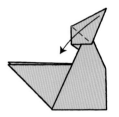

15 Fold the first layer back as far as it will go.

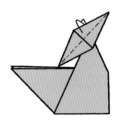

16 Mountain-fold the upper half of the head behind.

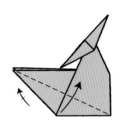

17 Fold both wings over between the two corners.

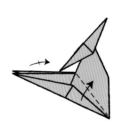

18 Fold the wings forward slightly.

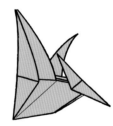

19 The pteranodon is finished.

*t*his design makes good use of reverse folds. The best way to understand these is to make them, then unfold them and look at how the creases work. They are all made here using pre-creases - the crease you need is put in first, then it is reversed. When you are more experienced at origami, you can often make the reverse folds directly without a pre-crease.

creative tips

You can curl the outer edges of the wings to make your flying dinosaur look more lifelike. If you fold the flap slightly further back in step 10, you can make the head longer, as shown in the photo.

18

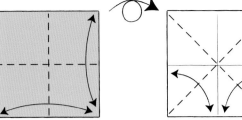 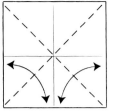 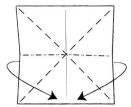 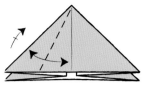 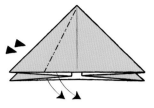

1 Start with a square, patterned side upward. Fold in half from side to opposite side, crease and unfold. Repeat the opposite way.

2 Turn the paper over. Crease both diagonals.

3 Use the creases shown to collapse the paper into a form known as the 'waterbomb' base.

4 Fold the left edge to the vertical centre. Crease firmly and unfold. Repeat on the matching flap underneath.

5 Inside-reverse the top flap, then repeat on the flap underneath.

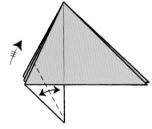 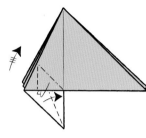 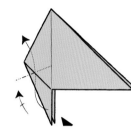 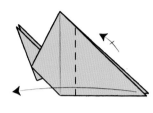 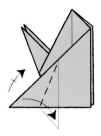

6 Fold the left plain edge to the vertical edge, crease and unfold. Repeat on the three matching flaps underneath.

7 Make a mountain fold to tuck the paper inside. As you press it in, make a valley fold which bisects the white flap underneath. Repeat three more times.

8 Reverse-fold the narrow point upwards and slightly forward, at right angles to the lower left edge. Repeat on the matching flap underneath.

9 Fold a flap to the left as shown. Repeat underneath.

10 Fold the upper leg to match the dotted line. Repeat underneath.

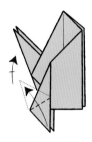    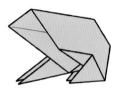

11 Form the feet by folding the lower corner to match the dotted line.

12 Fold over both layers at the corner. Crease and unfold.

13 Inside-reverse the corner.

14 Tuck the lower flap inside the pocket. Rotate the model to the final position.

15 The frog is finished.

*f*rogs, like penguins, are a highly popular subject for origami creators. The starting point for this model is the well-known 'waterbomb' base, which provides four flaps for legs and a corner for the head. Choosing a good base to start with allows the shape of the frog to be created without long-winded and complex techniques. Step 7 is an example of a 'swivel fold', in which some of the paper wraps underneath.

creative tip

There are many possibilities for placing the legs in different positions – see how many poses you can give your frog.

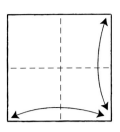

1 Start with the top of the box, plain side upward. Fold in half both ways, crease and unfold.

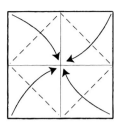

2 Fold all four corners to the centre of the paper.

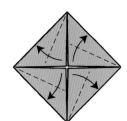

3 Fold an inside edge to the outside.

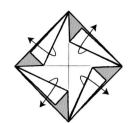

4 Unfold the double layers.

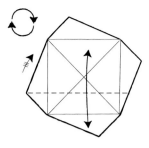

5 Rotate the paper slightly to this position. Make a valley fold starting at the widest corner on the left. Repeat on the three remaining sides.

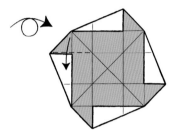

6 Turn the paper over. Fold over only the indicated area.

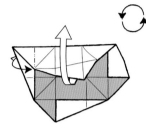

7 Reinforce the mountain crease shown. Unfold and repeat on each side.

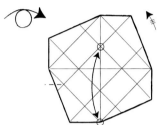

8 Turn the paper over and rotate it slightly. Fold the circled points to meet, creasing only the small section on the left.

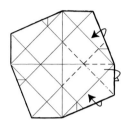

9 Using the creases shown, raise two sides and form the paper into three dimensions.

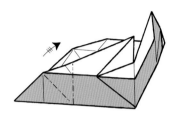

10 Repeat on the next corner and the remaining two sides.

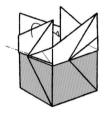

11 Carefully fold down a single flap.

12 Moving counter-clockwise, fold the next flap inwards.

13 Now fold the third flap inwards.

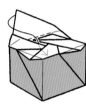

14 Carefully fold in the final corner, tucking it under the first flap.

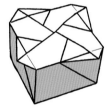

15 The box is finished.

*Y*ou might think that a simple box would be of little interest to a folder. However, many hundreds of origami boxes have been created and new ones keep appearing. Perhaps it's because the basic concept is so simple that people are keen to make their own. Inserting the final flap of the lid is slightly tricky, but after a couple of attempts you'll have no problems. It's a little like the way you fold the four flaps of a cardboard box under each other.

creative tip

In step 3, all of the edges must be folded the same way. However, you could fold them all the opposite way so the 'twist' of the lid goes in the opposite direction.

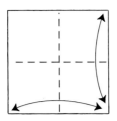

1 Start with a square, plain side upward. Fold in half from side to opposite side, crease and unfold. Repeat the opposite way.

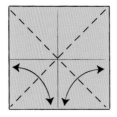

2 Turn the paper over. Crease both diagonals.

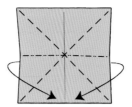

3 Use the creases shown to collapse the paper into a form known as the 'waterbomb' base.

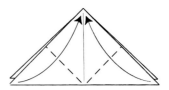

4 Fold each lower corner to the top corner.

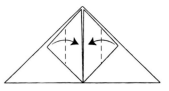

5 Fold the corners of the diamond-shaped section to the centre.

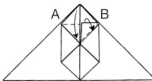

6 A fold the top corner to the centre. **B** fold the flap into the pocket.

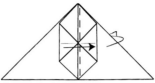

7 Fold the central section in half to the right. Fold the right lower flap behind to the left.

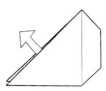

8 Gently ease out the hidden paper.

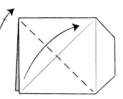

9 Fold the lower left corner to the opposite corner. Repeat underneath.

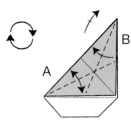

10 Rotate to this position. **A** Fold the lower edge to the upper left edge. Crease and unfold. **B** Fold the vertical edge to the upper left edge. Repeat underneath.

11 Fold the plain vertical edge to 45-degree crease, then unfold. Repeat underneath.

12 Inside-reverse using the crease you have just made.

13 Reverse the upper left corner inside to form the beak.

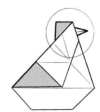

14 We now focus on the beak area.

15 Fold down the upper half of the beak for contrast.

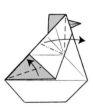

16 Put in the two valley folds. Carefully flatten to match the next diagram.

17 This is the result. Now we focus on the head area.

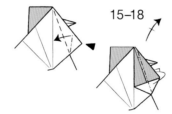

18 Fold the plain edge to match a hidden edge beneath, flattening the lower corner symmetrically. Fold the out half of the diamond shape behind. Repeat steps 15-18 on the underside.

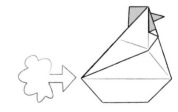

19 Carefully blow into the small hole at the rear end to inflate the chicken.

20 The chicken is finished.

Choosing interesting paper can make your models look more striking and, in this case, will provide good contrast for your different chicken 'parts'. As with the frog (see page 20), this design begins with the 'waterbomb' base, yet produces a very different result. When you reach step 16, the number of creases may look difficult, so always check the next drawing to see what you're aiming for and fold gently.

creative tip

Step 12 determines the basic shape of the head - try different folding angles to create other species.

rosetta

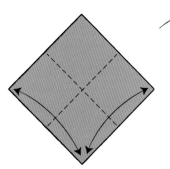

1 Start with a square, plain side upward. Fold in half from side to opposite side, crease and unfold. Repeat the opposite way.

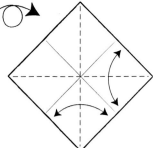

2 Turn the paper over. Crease both diagonals.

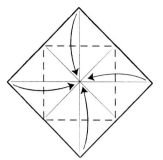

3 Fold all four corners to the centre.

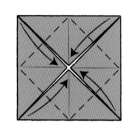

4 Again, fold all four corners to the centre.

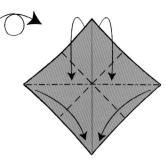

5 Turn the paper over. Use these creases to collapse the paper into a form known as a 'preliminary' base.

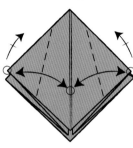

6 Fold the left and right corners to a point just below the centre of the paper. Crease and unfold. Repeat underneath.

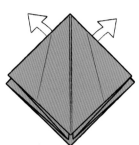

7 Unfold to match step 4.

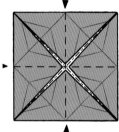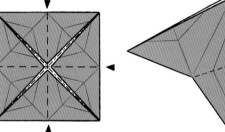

8 Fold into a loose three-dimensional shape using the crease shown.

9 Follow the creases shown very carefully to flatten the corner upwards.

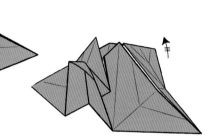

10 This is the result. Repeat on the three other corners.

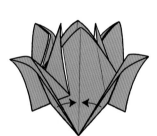

11 Fold the two flaps shown together.

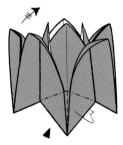

12 Holding the flaps in place, fold the lower corner underneath as far as you can. Repeat on the three similar areas.

13 The rosetta is finished.

*t*his beautiful origami rose comes from Italy. Folding four corners to the centre is called a 'blintz fold'. With this project we have a double blintz fold. You can see how step 6 produces symmetrical creases when the second blintz is unfolded, shown at step 8. You may find step 9 tricky at first, because the model is in three dimensions (it won't lie flat), but make sure every crease is exactly as shown. When you reach step 10, unfold and refold so you understand exactly how it works before repeating on the three other corners.

Creative tips

If you manage to complete this model, you already have creative skills. Just concentrate on making the most beautiful example you can.

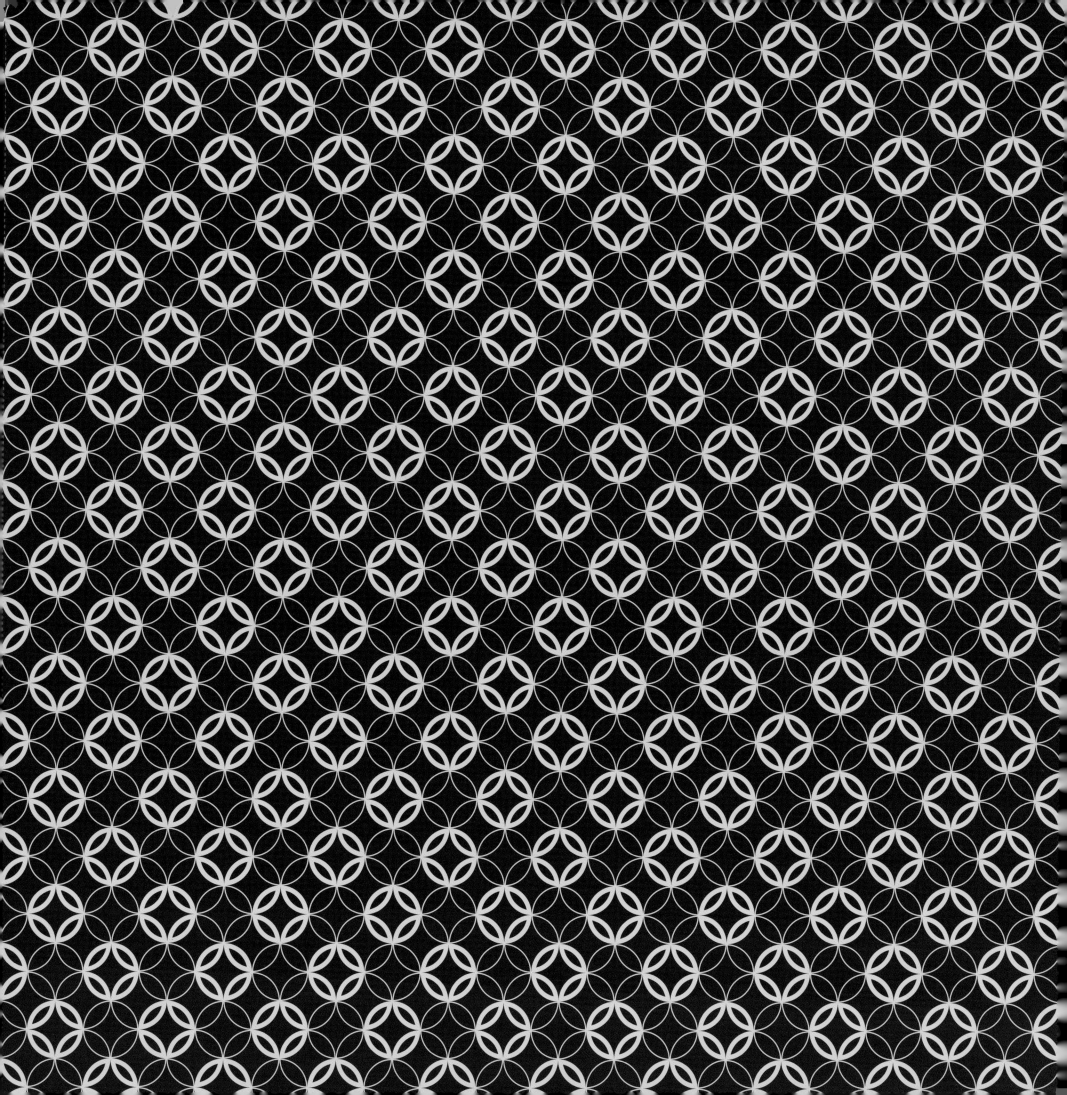